Dumbek Fever

Dumbek Instructional Kit

By Raquy Danziger

Jordan Press

Free Updates!
You can receive new compositions and rhythms via e-mail at no cost! Just e-mail us at Raquy@Raquy.Com and write as subject: "I want to receive updates."

Additional copies of "Dumbek Fever" may be purchased through **WWW.RAQUY.COM**

Jordan Press – Brooklyn Branch
136 South 2nd, Apt B5
Brooklyn, NY 11211

Photographs, Cover Art and DVD Filming by Natalia Perlaza
Cover Illustration by Raquy Danziger
Inside Photo by Sarah Skinner and Kevin Fox
Audio Tracks Recorded and Edited by Liron Peled
Video Edited by Lena Marvin

Special Thanks to:
Fishky, Natalia, Shlum, Eema, Aba, Marjorie, Linda and Elana

About This Kit

This is an interactive multimedia kit designed to teach the techniques and rhythms of dumbek playing. It does not require a musical background. The style presented is a combination of Arabic and Turkish drumming techniques and works best on the Egyptian style ("Alexandria") dumbek with the rounded rim (see page 10). The book covers traditional rhythms, solos, drum compositions and accompaniment of both songs and belly dance.

This kit is divided into two main sections.

Level I

"Instruction" Half of the Book + Enclosed DVD

A breakdown of the main hits and rhythms.

Level II

"Practice" Half of the Book + Enclosed CD

A thorough transcription of dumbek rhythms, solo phrases and compositions using the techniques presented in the first half of the book. Each segment in this section can be heard in the "Practice with Raquy" CD so that you can practice along.

Table of Contents

Letter From The Author

I grew up in a family of classical musicians and had a traditional classical music education studying violin, viola and focusing on the piano. While I clearly had a talent for music and enjoyed practicing and performing, I couldn't imagine myself being happy as a member of an orchestra or as a classical pianist.

After college I wandered the world, exploring different cultures. My travels took me to India where I discovered hand drumming. In Varanase, a fascinating spiritual and cultural center, I took lessons in dolak, a two sided folk drum. I loved the long complex cycles, and the Indian way of vocalization and counting.

Afterwards, in Israel, I became interested in the dumbek, the drum indigenous to the Middle East. I had seen dumbeks all around, at beaches and parties, etc., but hadn't paid much attention to them because many people just bang on the drum. When this drum is not played with the proper sounds and just hit hard, it can actually sound offensive. It wasn't until I heard a master player producing all the magical subtle sounds that I realized how beautiful this instrument could be.

Oddly enough, my career as a Middle Eastern musician began, not in the Eastern hemisphere, but with my arrival in New York City. Here I discovered an exciting, vibrant scene of Middle Eastern music and dance with a seemingly endless stream of belly dancers and master musicians from all over the Middle East making music together. This genre proved to be fertile ground for a kind of musical United Nations. For example, one of my ensembles, *The Radio Istanbul Orchestra*, is composed of a Greek, a Turk, an Armenian, an Egyptian and an Israeli!

In Middle Eastern music, the musicians have endless creative license for variation and improvisation, and the musician and the audience are not separate entities as they are in classical music, but join together to create an intoxicating atmosphere of "Kef" (fun). The experience of playing Middle Eastern music was exhilarating for me. Never before had I played for an audience of people who were singing and clapping along and spontaneously getting up to belly dance, not to mention throwing dollar bills at the performers!

Possibly the biggest thrill of all was discovering the dumbek's magical power to attract people from every possible background and persuasion. My students include writers, doctors, choral conductors, Rabbis, rocket scientists and tango dancers.

We look forward to every new season when a group of us goes off together to the Catskill Mountains to practice and learn my latest compositions, which we present in concert when we return to NYC. Many of my students have become so passionate, involved and expert at drumming that they now have students of their own!

Dumbek Fever is spreading far and wide.

Welcome!

Raquy Danziger
Brooklyn, 2005

About the Dumbek

The dumbek is the goblet drum played all over the Middle East in nightclubs, weddings and on the streets. It is used to accompany folk, pop, and belly dance music. In Turkey you find Gypsy musicians everywhere, playing dumbek in the streets and cafes for tips.

In Egypt, wedding parties take to the streets accompanied by troupes of drummers led by a dumbek player. The dumbek is extremely popular and is usually associated with festivity and celebration.

In general, people from different countries have different ways of playing the dumbek, but these days many musicians travel and study abroad, so the styles are all blending together. For example, one of the greatest dumbek players today in Turkey, Misirli Ahmed, actually studied dumbek in Egypt. He also incorporated an Indian technique of dividing the hand in his dumbek playing, giving him unprecedented speed.

Although the dumbek is occasionally used in Arabic art music, many classical musicians don't like this drum, which, in the drum hierarchy, is thought of as lower class. I heard one great music master refer to the dumbek as an "Arabic Tank." Drums such as the riq (tambourine) or the frame drum are more commonly played in classical and religious music.

Frame Drum

Riq

Types of Dumbeks

The dumbek has different names in different countries:
Egypt – Tabla
Greece – Dumberleki
Israel and Turkey – Darbuka
Bulgaria - Tarambuka

The dumbek I use is from Egypt, and the technique taught in this book is designed for this drum. It's called the "Alexandria Dumbek" because the factory that produces them originated in the city of Alexandria, Egypt. Most professional drummers play this one. It is tunable, extremely sturdy and quite heavy. The skin is made of plastic and the body is made of metal. I like the four peg dumbek, which is somewhat smaller and higher pitched than the standard six peg.

Another kind of dumbek is Turkish style. It has a rim around the edge and is played with a technique based on snapping.

Egyptian Style   Turkish Style

Instruction – Level I

Instructional Video

The material from the book is also shown in the enclosed "Dumbek Instructional Video."

When reading a particular chapter, you can watch the corresponding chapter in the video.

How to Hold it

Most people put the dumbek diagonally over their left thigh. (Note: Throughout this book I will refer to the hands from the right-handed point of view. If you are left handed, do the opposite of what is written.)

I like to sit cross-legged on the floor, but most dumbek players sit in a chair. If you can sit cross-legged with your knees touching the ground, you can rest it on your foot.

How I Like to Sit

How Most Dumbek Players Sit

The elbow of your left hand should be resting on the back of the drum. Make sure that your wrist is not bent upward. The left fingers should be comfortably draped over the rim pointing to the right, and should only be on the rim, not touching the drum head at all.

Posture

Everyone's body is different, so you have to find a position that is right for you. Make sure of the following:
- Your back is straight, your neck is straight and you are looking straight ahead.
- Your shoulders are relaxed.
- The drum is stable so that when you hit it, it doesn't move around.

If your body is touching the drum, the sound will be muffled. The drum should be away from your stomach. You actually don't need to see the head of the drum when you look down, so it can be in front of you.

Good posture makes a huge difference in your playing. When I am sitting correctly, I feel as though my body is a vessel channeling energy from above which flows down through my body and out from my wrists into the drum. If my upper body is bent or tense in any way, the energy cannot flow. Allowing the energy to flow through you allows you to play long, hard and fast without getting tired.

How Not to Sit

The Notation

I created the notation system used in this book based on the Indian notation system. It can easily be read by those who aren't familiar with Western musical notation, and it works well for Middle Eastern rhythms.

The system is based on underlines, each underline representing one beat.

The Notation Key

D = Dum (Right Hand Low Hit)

T = Tek (Right Hand Rim Hit)

K = Ka (Left Hand Rim Hit)

P = Pop

S = Slap

~ = Left Hand Finger Roll

~ ~ = Right Hand then Left Hand Finger Roll.

* = Rest (silence)

B = Dum and Ka (Both) at same time

DD= Double Dum (When you have two consecutive Dums fast, you can play every other one with the left hand)

The location of the letter on the line determines when to play it.   Here is an example of one hit per beat:

<u> T   K   T   K   </u>

Here are two hits per beat. The second letter on each line goes on the second half of the beat, in other words, dividing it into two. It sounds twice as fast as the previous example:

<u> T K   T K   T K   T K </u>

If the beat has three equal letters on it, as in the following example, it is a triplet (the beat is divided into thirds):

TKT	KTK	TKT	KTK

Here are four hits per beat:

TKTK	TKTK	TKTK	TKTK

Here, each beat is divided into one half and two quarters:

T TK	T TK	T TK	T TK

The upper case letters signify a loud hit while the lower case letters are soft and ghost-like:

D k	k T	k k	T k

To get a better grasp of this system, put on a metronome at 70bpm. Tap the beats on the page one at a time, one beat per line at a steady pace, NO MATTER HOW MANY LETTERS ARE ON THAT LINE. At the same time, read out loud what is on the lines. For example the following example reads "Tek Ka Tek Ka."

T	K	T	K
T K	T K	T K	T K

Tapping the beats and chanting the rhythm is a great way of internalizing the rhythm before you try playing it.

Interesting Note:

Because rhythms function in cyclical patterns that always return to the beginning it is more accurate to notate the rhythms in a circle, though I don't do it for practical reasons. However it's nice to visualize the rhythms in that way. This is what a rhythm would look like written in a circle starting from the top middle (12:00 on the clock).

Baladi Written in a Circle

Taking this concept even further, the most accurate way of thinking of rhythm is more like a spiral, because although the rhythm is going back to the beginning each time, it goes forward in time , making a spiral like this:

16

The Basic Hits – Dum, Tek and Ka

While the dumbek is capable of producing many different sounds, most of the traditional rhythms have simple versions that can be played using only the three basic hits – the Dum, the Tek and the Ka.

Dum

Dum is the lowest sound on the drum. Make your right hand flat like a solid sheet with no spaces in between the fingers. Hit the drum with the top part of the hand so that the palm falls in between the rim and the center and your knuckles line up with the rim of the drum. If your hand stays on the drum head after you hit it, the sound won't resonate, so make sure you bounce off softly. If you hit it too hard, there will be unwanted high sounds. The Dum should be a pure, low sound.

Dum Preparation

Dum Hit

Tek

Tek is the right hand high sound produced by hitting the drum where the rim meets the head with three straight open middle fingers. The fingers should make contact with the rim at a 30° angel.

Tek Preparation

Tek Hit

Dum and Tek Pointers:
- You need to have your fingers together for the Dum and spread apart for the Tek.
- While the Dum bounces off the drum, the hand can stay on the rim after you play the Tek.
- The Tek should sound as high as possible. The correct sound is ringy and almost bell-like.

Rhythms with Dum and Tek

Here are some simple rhythms you can play only using only the right hand hits, Dum and Tek. Later on, you will play more filled-in versions of these rhythms using additional hits:

Sneaky Greeky

D	T T	D	T
D T	T T	D	T

Zaar

D	* T	D	T

Maksum

D   T   *   T   D   *   T   *

Baladi

D   D   *   T   D   *   T   *

Chiftetelli

D   T T   * T   T   D   D   T   *

Samai

D   *   T   T   *   D   D   T   *   *

Debke

D   D   D   *   T   D   *   T   D   *   T   *

Ka

Of the three basic hits, the Ka poses the biggest challenge for rank beginners.

I count the fingers on each hand as thumb, 1, 2, 3.

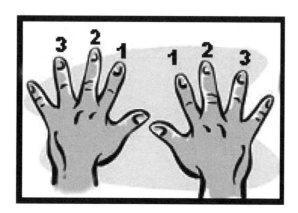

With your elbow resting on the back of the drum, raise your left hand about one inch up from the drum, as though you want to show your palm to someone facing you. This is the "preparation" position. The hand then falls towards your other hand, the tip of the third finger hits the line dividing the head and the rim and lands in the "resting" position with all fingers resting on the rim and NOT touching the drum head at all.

Ka Preparation

Ka Hit

Some people just cannot get a sound at first. However, everyone eventually gets it and they all say the same thing – "My Goodness, it's so easy!" Your hand needs to be completely relaxed to play a good Ka. There should be nothing forced about the motion. The more tension you have, the harder it is to make a sound.

The Tek and the Ka should be high and ringy, and should sound as similar to each other as possible. If they sound different from each other it is possible that the drum is out of tune. (See page 53 on tuning your drum.)

Switching

It is important to be as efficient as possible with your motions when playing the dumbek. If you avoid making unnecessary motions, eventually you will be able to play fast. So when you are playing one hand, you should be getting the other hand ready.

I define two positions for each hand as the "preparation" position and the '"resting" position. For each "preparation" position the person facing you should see the palm of your hand. The "resting" position should be very relaxed.
As soon as you move to make one hit, move the opposite hand to the "preparation" position and vice versa. I call this "switching."

When you play Tek Ka Tek Ka, the person facing you should always be able to see one of your palms. This goes for the Dum also. When you play the Dum or Tek, the Ka hand should shoot up and get into the "preparation" position. When you play the Ka, the Dum/ Tek hand should shoot out into the "preparation" position. Of course, when you start to play fast, the motion will become smaller, but in the beginning do it slowly enough to make the complete motion so that your body can learn that movement correctly.

Tek with Ka Preparing

Ka with Tek Preparing

Exercise – Make sure you're switching!

D	K	T	K

D K	T K	D K	T K

Traditional Rhythms w/ Basic Hits

The following are some traditional dumbek rhythms commonly used in Middle Eastern music and belly dancing. Try playing them in the metronome tempos indicated (see page 32 on playing with a metronome).

Baladi – 110 bpm
Baladi means "common" or "of the country." This Egyptian rhythm is popular with belly dancers.

D	D	TK	T	D	TK	T	TK

Maksum – 140 bpm
Most Middle Eastern pop, folk and dance songs are in Maksum.

D	T	K	T	D	K	T	TK

Maksum with Variation – 140 bpm

D	T	K	T	D	K	T	TK

D K	D	K	T	D	K	T	TK

Masmudi – 100 bpm

The Masmudi is a less frequently used rhythm. There aren't too many songs that are only in Masmudi. It usually makes a brief appearance for one or two rounds in Maksum based songs. It is popular with belly dancers and I often use it in belly dance drum solos.

2 Dum Masmudi – 100 bpm

D	T K	D	T K	T K	T K	T	T K

D	T K	T K	T	T K	T K	T	T K

3 Dum Masmudi –100 bpm

D	T K	D	T K	D	T K	T	T K
D	T K	T K	T	T K	T K	T	T K

Raquy Masmudi –100 bpm

D	T K	D	T K	D	T K	T	T K
D	T K	T K	T	T K	T K	T	T K
D	D	D	D	D	T K	T	T K
D	T K	T K	T	T K	T K	T	T K

Malfuf – 90 bpm

Malfuf means "wrapped around". The Malfuf is the most universal of the Arabic rhythms – there are versions of it in Latin, African, Irish and Indian music. Therefore, if you are jamming with non-Middle Eastern players, you will find the Malfuf popping up everywhere. What characterizes the Malfuf is that there are 8 fast hits, and the accents are **1** 2 3 **1** 2 3 **1** 2, so even though it fits into a cycle of 8, it feels lopsided and extremely groovy. People find it difficult to play the double Kas at a fast tempo. The secret is to play the Kas so softly that you barely hear them. Totally relax the hand and just lightly tap, so that the main hits stand out and you don't get tired.

D k	k T	k k	T k

Zaar – 90 bpm

This rhythm is used in Sufi trance ceremonies. Often it starts slowly and accelerates to a frenzy. It's also a popular rhythm for belly dancers. They either throw their heads around or spin to this rhythm.

D	* K	D	T	x3
D K	* K	D	T	x1

Chiftetelli – 90 bpm

This is the slow sensual rhythm where the belly dancer comes out with candles or veils.

D	*	K	T	*	K	T	T K
D	K	D	K	T	*	T	K

Wahda – 90 bpm

This rhythm is called Wahda because there is only one Dum. Wahda is used in classical Arabic music. In songs, the verses are often in Wahda while the refrain is in Maksum.

D   t k   t k   T   t k   t k   T   t k

4 Dum Saiidi – 100 bpm

The only difference between the Baladi and the Saiidi is the Saiidi's extra Dum on the 4th beat. As a result this rhythm feels heavier than the Baladi and can be played in a slower tempo. The Saiidi is great for dancers and is an instant crowd pleaser. I find that audiences go wild over it.

D   D   T K   D   D   T K   T   T K

3 Dum Saiidi – 100bpm

T K   D   T K   D   D   T K   T   T K

Bambi –100 bpm

This quirky rhythm is also used in Arabic classical music. I find it mysterious and suspenseful.

D k   k T   k k   T k   k T   k k   D   D

Switching Between Rhythms

Many songs switch back and forth between the above rhythms, while keeping the same pulse. Try switching between the following:

Maksum and Masmudi

D	T	K	T	D	K	T	TK	X2

D	T K	D	T K	D	T K	T	T K
D	T K	T K	T	T K	T K	T	T K

Maksum and Chiftetelli

D	T	K	T	D	K	T	T K	X4

D	*	K	T	*	K	T	TK	
D	K	D	K	T	*	T	K	X2

27

Wahda and Malfuf

D   tk   tk   T   tk   tk   T   tk   X2

D k   k T   k k   T k   X4

Malfuf and Baladi

D k   k T   k k   T k   X4

D   D   T K   T   D   T K   T   T K   X2

Fast Maksum and Baladi

D T   K T   D K   T TK   X4

D   D   T K   T   D   T K   T   T K   X2

Malfuf and Saiidi

D k   k T   k k   T k   X4

D   D   T K   D   D   T K   T   T K   X2

Solo Phrases

Soloing is like speaking or telling a story.

Solo phrases can be played over rhythms such as Maksum, Baladi or Malfuf. Every dumbek player needs to collect a database of solo phrase. The more you have, the more versatile your playing. You can practice these with a metronome, but it's more fun to have a friend hold down a rhythm for you. Here are some ideas, but it is never too early to try making up your own. Your original solo phrases will eventually define your own "voice." When practicing, try repeating each phrase four times. This will prepare you for playing a belly dance drum solo (see page 50).

TKT   K   TKT   K   TKT   K   T   *   X4

T   TK   T   TK   TK   TK   T   TK   X4

TKT   K   TK   TK   TKT   K   TK   TK   X4

TKT   KTK   TK   TK   TKT   KTK   T   *   X4

Odd Rhythms

One of my favorite things about Middle Eastern music is the extensive use of rhythms in odd time signatures. For example, in Turkey there are many songs and folk dances that are in 9s and 7s. The first time I played for a Turkish audience I was surprised to see the entire audience clapping along to the 9 beat rhythm we were playing!

Karsilama
The Turkish 9 beat rhythm called Karsilama is divided like this: 2+2+2+3. Here is a basic way to play it:

D	t k	T	t k	D	t k	T	T	t k

Gypsy Karsilama
The Gypsies do some very interesting variations with this rhythm. The following is an example of what the Gypsy drummer often plays when the song goes into a solo section. It is a powerful groove, especially when the other rhythm instruments follow the same pattern:

D	*	D	*	T K	T K	T K	T	T K
D	D	D	*	T K	T K	T K	T	T K

Seido Karsilama
Here is a syncopated version of the Karsilama, usually played in slower tempos. Seido is a Macedonian Gypsy dumbek player living in NYC.

D	T K	D K	* K	T	T K	D K	T	T K

Laaz

The Laaz is a popular seven beat rhythm from the Black Sea area. It's divided like this: 2+2+3

<u>D</u> <u>k</u> <u>T</u> <u>k</u> <u>D</u> <u>k</u> <u>k</u>

Subway Rhythm

I composed a song that takes the Laz rhythm structure and then plays it backwards so that you get a 14 beat cycle divided into 2+2+3+3+2+2. When I first moved to New York, this was very popular in the subway where I used to play.

<u>D</u> <u>k</u> <u>T</u> <u>k</u> <u>D</u> <u>k</u> <u>k</u> <u>D</u> <u>k</u> <u>k</u> <u>D</u> <u>k</u> <u>T</u> <u>k</u>

Samai

Classical Arabic Rhythm

<u>D</u> <u>t k</u> <u>T</u> <u>T</u> <u>t k</u> <u>D</u> <u>D</u> <u>T</u> <u>t k</u> <u>t k</u>

Kalamatianos

Greek Rhythm

<u>D</u> <u>t k</u> <u>t k</u> <u>D</u> <u>t k</u> <u>T</u> <u>t k</u>

Debke

Lebanese Line Dance for Men

<u>D</u> <u>D</u> <u>D</u> <u>t k</u> <u>T</u> <u>D</u> <u>t k</u> <u>T</u> <u>D</u> <u>t k</u> <u>T</u> <u>t k</u>

Playing with a Metronome

I do almost all of my practicing with a metronome. A metronome is a machine that clicks out a steady beat. You can buy one in any music store. You can change the speed of the clicks to whatever tempo you choose. The speed of the clicks is called "BPM" (beats per minute). When using the metronome with this notation, one click equals one underline.

My Metronome

Dividing Time

Drummers divide time with the sounds of their drum. The following is a basic exercise in dividing time that any drummer should be able to do. Take a period of time (called a "beat") and practice dividing it into 1, 2, 3, 4, 5 and 6. This exercise is never ending, and the more advanced you get, the more you can divide the beat.

ALWAYS do this exercise with a metronome. Set the metronome to 70 bpm. Play each line twice and then without stopping, go to the next line. When you reach the last line, go back down and end at the first line.

If you do this exercise well, you will notice that you can't hear the metronome, because your hit is so in sync with the click that it covers it up!

Time Exercise

T	K	T	K	x2
TK	TK	TK	TK	x2
TKT	KTK	TKT	KTK	x2
TKTK	TKTK	TKTK	TKTK	x2
TKTKT	KTKTK	TKTKT	KTKTK	x2
TKTKTK	TKTKTK	TKTKTK	TKTKTK	x2

The Time Exercise is more for your brain than for technique. Therefore, it is just as useful to chant it as it is to play it. Another way to practice this is to use your footsteps to tap out the beat and chant the exercise when you are walking down the street. Practicing to your footsteps while you are walking is extremely useful. Because your whole body is moving in that pace, you can really feel the beat.

Note: Notice that when you are dividing the beat into even numbers (2,4,etc.) each beat starts on the right hand. When you divide the beat into odd numbers (1,3,5,ect.), every other beat starts on the left hand. This awareness will come in handy later on when you start playing long rolls.

Another Note: Unlike exercises for technique, this one should not speed up. On the contrary, the better you get at this exercise, the slower you should do it, because the more time you have to deal with, the harder it is to divide.

Pop

The Pop is a sound made by playing the Ka while pressing down on the drum head with the right hand. The result is a very high poppy sound. I've seen many ways of pressing with the right hand (side of the hand, fist, and one finger), each one producing slightly different sounds. I would recommend starting with the side of the hand. Make your right hand parallel to the ground facing up, and press it into the drum (like a karate chop).

Pop Preparation

Pop Hit

By pressing down on different areas of the dumbek head, you can change the pitch of the Pop. The closer you press to the rim the higher the sound. Also, the harder you press the higher the sound. Try playing a scale by moving the right hand gradually up the head . You can even play simple melodies (try "Happy Birthday to You" for example). The Pop is extremely useful in soloing.

Exercise

P	K	P	K

D	K	P	K

Traditional Rhythms with Pops

Malfuf for Belly Dancers

D k	k T	k k	T k	x3
D	D	P	*	x1

Maksum with Variation

D	P	K	P	D	K	P	T K
D K	D	K	P	D	K	P	T K

Chiftetelli

D	*	K	T	*	K	T	T K
D	K	D	K	P	*	T	K

Solo Phrases with Pops

TKT	K	P	*	TKT	K	P	*
TKT	K	P	K	TKT	K	P	*

P	K	P	K	TKT	K	TKT	K
P	K	P	K	TKT	K	TKT	K

P	K	K	P	K	K	P	K
K	P	K	K	D	K	P	*

TKT	K	P	TKT	K	P	TKT	K
P	TKT	K	P	D	K	P	*

Slap

The Slap is used in Middle Eastern party music. It is the loudest sound on the dumbek and can be painful to those sitting nearby, but it is also possible to play a beautiful soft Slap. It has a high and crispy sound.

I've seen a few different kinds of Slaps, but I'll describe the one that I use the most. Cup your right hand and slap it into the drum so that only the bottom side of the hand and the fingertips are touching the skin. Your hand will end up in the shape of a tent. Instead of bouncing off, like you do with the Dum, stick to the drum. The result is a crisp, high pitched slapping sound that is distinctly different from the Tek. When you get it, you will know it. Whenever my students first succeed in producing a Slap, it is cause for great excitement and celebration.

Slap Preparation   **Slap Hit**

Here is an exercise to practice the Slap. Make sure that the Dum is releasing the vibrations and that the Slap is closing them. Try to make the Slap and the Tek sound different.

D	S	T	S

Rhythms with Slaps

Maksum

D	S	K	S	D	K	S	T K

Maksum with Variation

D	S	K	S	D	K	S	T K
D K	S	K	S	D	K	S	T K

Malfuf

D k	k S	k k	S k	X3
D	D	P	*	X1

Baladi

D	D	T K	S	D	T K	S	T K

You can play a Pop immediately after a Slap by keeping your hand on the drum after the Slap. Then the Pop becomes a Slap! Try the following:

Zafir Malfuf (B is Dum and Ka at the same time)

B	K S	P	S K
D K	K S	P	S

Finger Roll

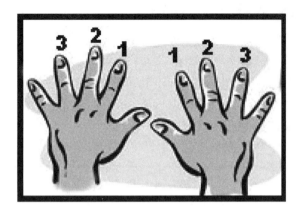

In this chapter I will present the left hand Finger Roll which acts as an ornament for a right hand hit. I find the left hand Finger Roll to be much more useful than that of the right hand, because the Roll decorates a main hit, and most main hits are played with the right hand. Therefore the Roll is usually played with the left hand.

Playing the Roll is one case where your left elbow is not resting on the drum but is slightly elevated. I brace my left thumb on the rim and fingers 1-3 are hanging down and STRAIGHT like STICKS.

The fingers can either hit the drum an inch or so down from the rim for a closed sound or right near the rim for a higher more ring-y sound. Try it in both places. Here is a preliminary exercise:

321	T	321	D	321	T	321	D

To play a Roll you need to cultivate strength and independence in your fingers. When I do many finger exercises, I begin to feel as if each of my fingers has a brain of its own and that I have 10 little intelligent beings on my hands!

Here is a great finger exercise that you can practice without a drum. All you need is a surface. The point is to take turns accenting each of the three fingers. The bold number represents the one that gets accented. Try this exercise with both hands, because eventually you will use it with your right hand as well:

3   2   1   **3**   2   1

3   **2**   1   3   **2**   1

3   2   **1**   3   2   **1**

Putting the Roll into Context

When you begin to have strength and independence in your fingers, you will be ready to put the roll into context.

For this you have to get used to another kind of "switching." There are two different left hand positions – one for the Roll and one for the Ka, which we learned earlier.

For the Roll - Thumb is braced on the rim, fingers are straight and facing down, and elbow is raised.
For the Ka – Regular Ka position.

While the right hand is playing, the left hand switches positions.

<u>321</u>   <u>T</u>   <u>K</u>   <u>T</u>

For the above exercise:
- The hand starts in the Roll position – Play the Roll.
- When you play the Tek, take the opportunity to switch the left hand position, putting elbow down and palm up.
- Play the Ka
- When the next Tek is playing, switch the left hand to the first "preparation" position.

Roll Position

Ka Position

Make sure that each of the fingers is playing separately and evenly. Otherwise your Roll will sound like mush.

When you are first practicing the Roll, make it a triplet. Eventually, when it gets strong, you can make it shorter and more ornament-like.

Now try the same exercise adding a Dum:

321   D   K   T   321   T   K   T

From now on I will notate the left hand 321 finger roll as ~.

Now you are ready to play a rhythm with Rolls. Here is a popular Anatolian rhythm:

D   ~   T   K

When inserting Finger Rolls into a rhythm, you can put one before any right hand hit as long as there is nothing on the second half of the previous beat (because that is where the Roll needs to go).

Be careful to keep the Roll in its proper place! The Roll is merely an ornament of the Tek or Dum, so always focus your attention on the note that is being ornamented, and make sure it is on time.

Rhythms with Finger Rolls

Baladi

D   D ~   T K   T   D ~   T K   T ~   T K

Masmudi

D ~   T K   D ~   T K   T K   T K   T ~   T K
D ~   T K   T K   T ~   T K   T K   T ~   T K

Karsilama

D ~   T K   T ~   T K   D ~   T K   T   T ~   T K

Chiftetelli

D ~   T K   *K   T TK   D K   D K   P ~   T K

Kalamatianos

D ~   T K   T K   D ~   T K   T ~   T K

Saiidi + Variation

T K   D ~   T K   D   D ~   T K   S ~   T K
D   S   D   D   D ~   T K   S ~   T K

Solo Phrases with Rolls

Practice each one four times:

T ~	T K	T ~	T K	T ~	T K	T ~	T K
T ~	T K	T ~	T K	D	K	P	*

T ~	T K	* K	T ~	T K	* K	T ~	T K
* K	T~	TK	*K	D	D	P	*

T ~	T K	T K	T ~	T K	T K	T ~	T K
T K	T ~	T K	T K	D	K	P	*

T K	T ~	T K	T ~	T K	T K	T	T ~
T K	T ~	T K	T ~	T K	T K	T	T ~

Two Hand Finger Rolls

Just as the one-hand Finger Roll can take up a half a beat, the two-hand Finger Roll can take up a whole beat. I always start this roll with my right hand, so when I write ~ ~, first play 321 on the right hand and then 321 on the left hand.

Two Hand Finger Roll

Exercise

~ ~	TK	~ ~	TK
D K	~ ~	T K	~ ~

Rhythms with Double Finger Rolls

Chiftetelli

D	~~	T	P	~~	T	P	T K
D	K	D	K	P	~~	T	K

Samai

D~~	t k	T	P~~	t k	D k	D	P~~	tktk	t k

Persian

D	~ ~	T K	D	P	*
T	~ ~	T K	D	P	*
D	~ ~	T K	D K	K D	K K
T	~ ~	T K	D	P	*

Rhumba

D	T	~ ~	T	D	~ ~	T	~ ~

Roll-y Karsilama

D	~ ~	T	~ ~	D	~ ~	T	T	~ ~

Solos with Double Finger Rolls

D	K	~	~	T	K	~	~
T	K	~	~	T	K	~	~

D	K	~	~	T	K	D	K
~	~	T	K	D	*	P	*

Practicing Tek Ka Rolls

Being able to roll for a long time is essential for a dumbek player. When you play in Middle Eastern clubs, many of the songs end with a long roll which may go on and on. If you are tense when you begin the roll you are doomed, because it is almost impossible to relax once your muscles have tensed up. The secret is to start relaxed and let the roll flow through you.

Here is an exercise I use to practice being relaxed when I play a roll. You must be sitting up straight and holding the dumbek in a stable way so that it doesn't move while you hit it. Make sure your back is straight and your limbs are relaxed. Looking straight ahead, your head should be aligned with your neck. Make sure you are breathing and **completely comfortable**.

Raise your hands just enough to play Tek and Ka. Play softly and rapidly, but make sure nothing changes in the tension of your body (the only thing moving should be your wrists.) Gradually get louder, making sure you are breathing steadily and that your face, arms and shoulder area are still completely relaxed.

Inevitably, if you go on for long enough you will start to feel tension in your arms, but the object is to keep that from happening for as long as possible. As soon as you begin feeling tension, stop, stretch, breathe and start again. Each time you do this, you will be able to last longer without getting tense. If you are relaxed enough, you will be able to play very loud and very fast without feeling it at all! It's as if your body is a vessel, receiving energy from above and channeling it through the wrists and into the drum. This is the state you should strive to be in whenever you play. You will reach an ecstatic feeling of freedom and control that will allow you to execute technical feats with an ease and grace you never dreamed possible.

The Role of the Dumbek Player

The main role of the dumbek player is that of accompanist. Most of the time, the dumbek accompanies instruments such as the oud, the clarinet, or the kanun. A great drummer always thinks about the song first, providing only what the song requires in the best way possible. This can sometimes mean holding a very simple beat. The most successful drummers are the ones who strive to make the other musicians sound good.

Oud

Clarinet

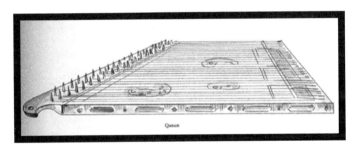

Kanun

My favorite way to learn is to play with more experienced musicians. Have them tell you the name of the rhythm before each song begins and watch them carefully for changes. Be alert. There are often sudden breaks in Middle Eastern music that you will miss if you're spacing out!

If you accompany a singer, your volume should drop considerably when he/she is singing, especially in the verses. The refrains can get somewhat louder and the instrumental parts can be the loudest.

The best way to become good at accompanying is to listen to as much Middle Eastern music as possible.

When you listen, try to identify the rhythms. Most of the rhythms you will hear are covered in this book.

After you listen to a recording a few times and start getting the feel of the song, try playing along, but play softly enough so that you can still hear the melody and the other drummers. You'll probably find it challenging to keep up with the fast tempos, but even if you hold a simple version of the rhythm with the right hand only, you will get a feel for the music.

My favorite kinds of music for dumbek are:

- Instrumental music from Lebanon, Egypt or Turkey
- Belly Dance music
- Turkish Gypsy music
- Middle Eastern percussion troupes.

You also hear lots of dumbek in pop and folk music.

Playing for Belly Dancers

Belly dance is a Middle Eastern dance form that was spread throughout the Middle East by Gypsies. Originally connected to fertility rights, belly dance has now become standard entertainment in restaurants, parties and nightclubs. It also appears in Middle Eastern households where you may find the women dancing in celebration of a girl about to be married.

Dumbek and belly dancing go together. Most gigs for dumbek players involve belly dancing. The hits of the drum and the sharp movements of the belly dancer's hips have a strong connection, often mimicking each other. Many belly dancers play rhythms on finger symbols called zils while they dance.

The following are instruments typically used in belly dance music. Ensembles range in size from oud and dumbek duet to a big band with many musicians.
- Oud
- Kanun
- Clarinet, Nay (Arabic Flute) or Violin as the lead
- Drums – Dumbek, Riq, Bass Dumbek and Frame Drum

The following is an example of a traditional belly dance set:
- Upbeat entrance song
- Rhumba, usually played like a simple slow Maksum
- Heavy Baladi or Saiidi
- Slow sensual song in Chiftetelli
- Drum solo
- Karsilama (9 beat rhythm) for exit

The Drum Solo

However nervous you are about playing your drum solo for a dancer, she is probably twice as nervous. Many dancers are terrified of the drum solo. As far as the other songs in the set, the dancers know what to expect, but with the drum solo, they are completely at the mercy of the drummer. No matter how good the drummer is, if he or she doesn't play a "dancer friendly" solo, the dancer will look foolish.

After years of playing for dancers, I have come to realize that there is a big difference between a drum solo and a belly dance drum solo. It is possible to play a drum solo that's technically and musically phenomenal, but would be a terrible solo to dance to. The following chapter will lay down guidelines for playing a good belly dance drum solo.

Basic Rules

- Base your solo on belly dance rhythms (for example Baladi, Saiidi, Maksum, Malfuf, Bambi, Masmudi, Chiftetelli, Zaar)

- Do not stray too far from the beat in your variations. The downbeat should be obvious to the dancer.

- If you do a solo phrase, repeat it four times so that the dancer will have a few chances to catch it.

It is easiest to play a drum solo for a dancer if you have another percussion instrument such as a riq, bendir or bass dumbek holding down the beat so that you can be free to solo. If there isn't a second percussionist, ask one of the musicians in the band to pick up a frame drum and hold a simple beat for you. It makes the solo much richer, easier and better. My favorite accompanying drum when I play a solo is the bass dumbek. It is important that the bass drum play very simply to leave space for the solo dumbek.

Bass Dumbek

There are certain rhythms over which you can solo, playing any phrase you choose. Other rhythms lend themselves more to variation.

Here are rhythms that you should play and then vary, keeping their basic structures:
- Masmudi
- Chiftetelli
- Bambi
- Zaar

Here are rhythms over which you can solo. Set the groove and then go off!
- Baladi
- Saiidi
- Maksum
- Malfuf

In my solos I like to have varying sections that set different moods, and then build to a frenzy for the ending.

How to Make the Dancer Happy:

- Talk to the dancer before the set and find out if there is anything special she would like you to do in the solo

- Pay attention and interact with the dancer

- Be flexible. Even if you have something planned out, if you see that the dancer isn't catching a rhythm or getting tired, change your plan to accommodate her. Once I was so oblivious to the dancer that she actually sat down next to me and started fanning herself so that I would get the hint that she was tired!

- Give her contrasts to work with such as soft and loud, busy and empty, fast and slow.

- If the dancer is good on the zils, give her space to play. Sometimes I play a solo phrase and then leave one phrase empty for her to respond on the zils – that makes for a nice dialogue.

- Keep in mind that a successful drum solo is one that makes the dancer look as good as possible, even if that means that you play simply. Save the wild stuff for your solos without a dancer.

For a typical belly dance drum solo, see page 92

Tuning the Drum
Frequently Asked Questions

Is my drum in tune?

It's important to make sure your drum is in tune, because you cannot get nice sounds if the drum is out of tune. A dumbek is in tune if the rim is the same pitch anywhere you hit it. To check this, hit the rim at each of the pegs and listen. If each pitch is the same, your drum is in tune. If not, you should tune it.

How do I tune it?

Usually the dumbek comes with an allen wrench for tuning. If not, bring your dumbek to any hardware store and they will give you an allen wrench that fits. The dumbek requires a metric allen wrench as opposed to a standard one.

Always tune each peg and then its opposite peg (as opposed to going around the circle.)

Do I want it lower or higher?

This is a matter of taste. I personally like my drum pitch to be quite high, so if the drum is out of tune, I'll tune the lower pegs up to match the higher pegs.

However, some dumbek players prefer the lower sound, in which case they would tune the higher pegs down to match the lower ones. If you want something in the middle, you can lower the high ones and raise the low ones gradually until they all match.

What if I can't get it in tune?

Sometimes this happens. Try changing the head. Loosen all the pegs until you can remove the rim and the head. Put on a new head and gradually tune it up, tuning each peg and its opposite peg.

What pitch should the Dum be?

The Alexandria dumbeks have a small tuning range in which they sound good. Usually the small four peg drums have a Dum in D and the bigger six peg drums have a Dum in C.

If you are accompanying music, you can choose which drum to play according to the key of the song. For example, a lot of Middle Eastern music is played in the key of D, which sounds very nice accompanied by the small dumbek with a Dum in D.

How often should I tune my drum?

Because all materials of the Alexandria dumbek are man-made, the tuning is not affected by the weather. Once you get it in tune, chances are it will stay that way for a long time.

Practice – Level II

Rhythms and Variations

| | Pg 56 | Tracks 1-63 |

Solo Section

Maksum	Pg 68	Track 64, 65
Malfuf	Pg 70	Track 66, 67
Baladi	Pg 72	Track 68, 69
Karsilama	Pg 74	Track 70, 71

Compositions

Naughty 9	Pg 78	Track 72
Shlum B-day	Pg 82	Track 73
Spring Fever	Pg 86	Track 74
Ein Sh'alla	Pg 88	Track 75

Belly Dance Drum Solo Minus Lead

| | Pg 92 | Track 76 |

Bonus Track

Raquy and the Cavemen playing "Nubian"

| From their album *Jordan.* | | Track 77 |

Practice CD

You can practice the material in this section along with the enclosed "Practice with Raquy" CD.
The track numbers of the CD are indicated next to each segment.

Rhythms and Variations

This section presents a thorough transcription of rhythms and variations that are useful to dumbek players.

Every rhythm and variation is written out and played on the "Practice with Raquy" CD. The number of times each segment is played is indicated next to the notes.

Practicing Tips:
You can jump to various track marks for specific rhythms.

For a real work-out, try playing along to the entire section! If you get lost, you can always refer to the track numbers to get back "on track"!

Rhythms with Variations

Baladi

Tr 1

Regular Baladi (8X)

D   D   T K   T   D   T K   T   T K

Tr 2

With Slaps (8X)

D   D   T K   S   D   T K   S   T K

Tr 3

With Rolls and Slaps (8X)

D   D ~   T K   S   D ~   T K   S ~   T K

Tr 4

With Triplets (8X)

D   D   KTK   S   D   KTK   S   KTK

Tr 5

With Quadruplets (8X)

D   D   TKTK   S   D   TKTK   S   TKTK

Maksum

Tr 6

Regular Maksum (8X)

D	T	K	T	D	K	T	T K

Tr 7

Maksum with Variation (8X)

D	T	K	T	D	K	T	T K
D K	D	K	T	D	K	T	T K

Tr 8

Maksum with Slaps (8X)

D	S	K	S	D	K	S	T K

Tr 9

Delicate Maksum with Pops and Roll (8X)

D	P	K	P	D ~	T K	T ~	T K
D K	D	K	P	D ~	T K	T ~	T K

Tr 10

Osama Maksum 1 (8X)

B	S	K	S	B	T K	S	K

Tr 11

Osama Maksum 2 (8X)

B	S	K	S	B	T K	S	K
D K	S	K	S K	D	K	TKT	K

Tr 12

Switching between Baladi and Maksum (4X)

D	D	T K	S	D	T K	S	T K	X2
D S	K S	D k	S TK	D S	k S	D K	S TK	X2

58

Malfuf Family

Tr 13

Regular Malfuf (4X)

D k	k T	k k	T k	X3
D	D	P	*	X1

Tr 14

Malfuf with Slaps (4X)

D k	k S	k k	S k	X3
D	D	S	*	X1

Tr 15

Serto (16X)

D	K T	*K	T K

Tr 16

Serto with rolls (16X)

D ~	T K	*K	T K

Tr 17

Shlum Malfuf (8X)

B	* S	K	S	D K	* S	K	S

Tr 18

Zafir Malfuf (8X)

B	K S	P	S K	D K	K S	P	S

Tr 19

Khaleedgi (16X)

D k	k D	k k	T K

Saiidi

Regular 4 Dum Saiidi (8X)

Tr 20

D	D	T K	D	D	T K	T	T K

3 Dum Saiidi (8X)

Tr 21

T K	D	T K	D	D	T K	T	T K

With Variation and Slaps (4X)

Tr 22

T K	D	T K	D	D	T K	S	T K
D	S	D	D	D	T K	S	T K

Figaro Saiidi (4X)

Tr 23

T K	D	T K	D	D	T K	S	T K
D	S	D	D	D	T K	S K	K S
K K	D	T K	D	D	T K	S	T K
D	S	D	D	D	T K	S	T K

Tr 24

Sick Saiidi (2X)

D	S	K D	D	D ~	T K	S ~	T K
S	D	K D	D	D ~	T K	S D	D D
D	S	K D	D	D ~	T K	S K	K S
K K	D	K D	D	D ~	T K	S D	D D
D	S	K D	D	D ~	T K	S ~	T K
S	D	K D	D	D ~	T K	S D	D D
D	S	K D	D	D ~	T K	S K	K S
*	D	K D	D	D ~	T K	S D	D D

Chiftetelli

Regular Chiftetelli (8X)

Tr 25

D	*	K	T	*	K	T	T K
D	K	D	K	T	*	T	K

With Pop (8X)

Tr 26

D	*	K	T	*	K	T	T K
D	K	D	K	P	*	T	K

With Pop and Rolls (8X)

Tr 27

D	~	T	K	*	K	T	T K
D	K	D	K	P	~	T	K

With Double Finger Rolls (8X)

Tr 28

D	~ ~	T	P	~ ~	T	P	T K
D	K	D	K	P	~ ~	T	K

With Long Roll (8X)

Tr 29

D	*	K	T	*	K	T	T K
D	K	D	K	P	*	tktk	tktk

Masmudi

Tr 30

Regular (8X)

D	T K	D	T K	T K	T K	T	T K
D	T K	T K	T	T K	T K	T	T K

3 Dum (8X)

Tr 31

D	T K	D	T K	D	T K	T	T K
D	T K	T K	T	T K	T K	T	T K

Raquy Masmudi (4X)

Tr 32

D	T K	D	T K	D	T K	T	T K
D	T K	T K	T	T K	T K	T	T K
D	D	D	D	D	T K	T	T K
D	T K	T K	T	T K	T K	T	T K

Masmudi with Rolls (8X)

Tr 33

D ˜	T K	D ˜	T K	T K	T K	T ˜	T K
D ˜	T K	T K	T ˜	T K	T K	T ˜	T K

Bambi (8X)

Tr 34   D k | k T | k k | T k | k T | k k | D | D

Kurdish (16X)

Tr 35   D | * k | D | D | T | * k | D | T

Busta Rhymes + Favorite (4X)

Tr 36   D | T K | D | T K | D K | K D | * | T K   X4

        D | D | D | D | D k | k S | k k | S k   X4

Fun (16X)

Tr 37   D k | k D | k k | T k | T k | k D | k k | T K

Anatolian (16X)

Tr 38   D ~ | T K | D ~ | T K

Zaar (8X)

Tr 39   D | * K | D | T   x3
        D K | * K | D | T   x1

Karache (8X)

Tr 40   T | * K | T | D   x3
        T K | * K | T | D   x1

Wahda (8X)

Tr 41   D | t k | t k | T | t k | t k | T | t k

Karsilama

Regular (8X)

Tr 42
D	T K	T	T K	D	T K	T	T	T K

With Slaps (8X)

Tr 43
D	T K	S	T K	D	T K	S	S	T K

With Left Hand Rolls (8X)

Tr 44
D ~	T K	T ~	T K	D ~	T K	T	T ~	T K

Double Hand Rolls (Very Rolly) (8X)

Tr 45
D	~ ~	T	~ ~	D	~ ~	T	T	~ ~

Gypsy Karsilama (8X)

Tr 46
D	*	D	*	T K	T K	T	T	T K
D	D	D	*	T K	T K	T	T	T K

Seido Karsilama (8X)

Tr 47
D ~	T K	D K	* K	T ~	T K	D K	T	T K

Kalamatianos (8X)

Tr 48
D	t k	t k	D	t k	T	t k

Kalamatianos with Rolls (8X)

Tr 49
D ~	t k	t k	D ~	t k	T ~	t k

Tr 50

Laaz (8X)

D	k	T	k	D	k	k	X3
D	*	D	*	P	*	*	X1

Tr 51

Laaz with Rolls (8X)

D	~	T	k	D	k	k	X3
D	*	D	*	P	*	*	X1

Tr 52

Çuçuna (pronounced George-una) (8X)

D	k	K	T	k	D	k	T	k	K

Tr 53

Samai (8X)

D	t k	T	T	t k	D	D	T	t k	t k

Tr 54

Fancy Samai (8X)

D~~	t k	T	P~~	t k	D k	D	P~~	tktk	t k

Tr 55

Moroccan 6 (8X)

D k	T k	T k	D k	k T	k k

Tr 56

Mach Mach 6 (8X)

S k	k S	D

Tr 57

Nubian (4X)

D	K D	* K	D	T	T K
T	K T	* K	D	T	T K
D K	K D	K K	D	T	T K
T K	K T	K K	D	T	T K

Tr 58

Persian Fast (8X)

D K	K D	K ~~	T K	K D	K ~~

65

Persian Medium (8X)

Tr 59

D	~ ~	T K	D	P	*
T	~ ~	T K	D	P	*

Tr 60

Persian Slow (2X)

D	*	~ ~	~ ~	T	K
D	*	P	*	*	*
T	*	~ ~	~ ~	T	K
D	*	P	*	*	~ ~

D	*	~ ~	~ ~	T	K
D	K	K	D	K	K
T	*	~ ~	~ ~	T	K
D	*	P	*	*	~ ~

Tr 61

Kopanitsa (Bulgarian 11) (8X)

D	k	T	k	D	k	k	D	k	T	k

Tr 62

Krivo Sadovkso (Bulgarian 13) (8X)

D	k	T	k	T	k	D	k	k	D	k	T	k

Bucimis (Bulgarian 15) (8X)

Tr 63

D	k	T	k	D	k	T	k	D	k	k	D	k	T	k

Solo Section

This section allows you to feel what it's like soloing over Maksum, Malfuf, Baladi and Karsilama grooves played by the bass dumbek and riq.

Practicing Tips:
In the CD, you can hear each two-line phrase played by the lead dumbek. Afterwards there is an empty phrase with only the backup groove playing. This is your chance to play the phrase! Each phrase is repeated twice.

Listen and then repeat each phrase twice before going on to the next one.

After each solo section, there is an entire backup track with no lead dumbek. You can make up your own solo and practice it over the bass drum and riq groove or you can use the same groove to practice the phrases on the previous page.

Try actually writing down some phrases in the "Make Up Your Own" page that you can practice over the backup groove.

Also, try improvising on the spot without preparing anything ahead of time.

For each 2 line phrase, listen and repeat twice.

S	*	S	*	S	*	S	*
T K	T K	T K	T K	D	K	P	*

*	T K	T K	T K	S	T K	T K	T K
S	T K	T K	T K	D	K	P	*

T K	T K	T K	T K	T K	T K	T K	T K
T K	T K	T K	T K	D	K	P	*

P	K	P	K	P	K	P	K
P	K	P	K	D	K	P	*

P	K	K	P	K	K	P	K
K	P	K	K	D	K	P	*

TKT	K	TKT	K	TKT	K	TKT	K
TKT	K	TKT	K	TKT	K	P	*

TKT	K	*	*	*	*	TKT	K
TKT	K	*	*	D K	T K	S	*

T ~	T K	T ~	T K	T ~	T K	T ~	T K
T ~	T K	T ~	T K	D K	T K	S	*

S	T K	T K	T K	S	T K	T K	T K
S	T K	T K	T K	D	K	P	*

P	*	P	*	D K	T K	S	TKT
K	TKT	K	T K	D K	T K	S	*

Make Up Your Own Maksum Solo   Track 65
Play your original phrases over the bass and riq groove!

Malfuf Solo   Track 66

For each 2 line phrase, listen and repeat twice.

S	T K	T K	T K	S	T K	T K	T K
S	T K	T K	T K	D	K	P	*

S	T K	S	T K	S	T K	S	T K
S	T K	S	T K	D K	T K	S	*

TKT	K	P	*	TKT	K	P	*
TKT	K	P	K	D K	T K	S	*

P	K	TKT	K	D	K	P	K
P	K	TKT	K	D	D	P	*

TKT	KTK	TKT	KTK	TKT	KTK	TKT	KTK
TKT	KTK	TKT	KTK	D	D	P	*

S	T K	TKT	KTK	S	T K	TKT	KTK
S	T K	TKT	KTK	D	D	P	*

TKT	KTK	TKT	KTK	TKT	KTK	TKT	KTK
TKT	KTK	TKT	KTK	TKT	KTK	S	*

T ~	T K	T K	T K	T ~	T K	T K	T K
T ~	T K	T K	T K	D	D	S	*

T K	K T	K K	T K	K T	K K	T K	K T
K K	T K	K T	K K	D ~	T K	S	*

S K	K S	K K	S K	K S	K K	S K	K S
K K	S K	K S	K K	D ~	T K	S	*

Make Up Your Own Malfuf Solo   Track 67
Play your original phrases over the bass and riq groove!

____ ____ ____ ____ ____ ____ ____ ____
____ ____ ____ ____ ____ ____ ____ ____

____ ____ ____ ____ ____ ____ ____ ____
____ ____ ____ ____ ____ ____ ____ ____

____ ____ ____ ____ ____ ____ ____ ____
____ ____ ____ ____ ____ ____ ____ ____

____ ____ ____ ____ ____ ____ ____ ____
____ ____ ____ ____ ____ ____ ____ ____

____ ____ ____ ____ ____ ____ ____ ____
____ ____ ____ ____ ____ ____ ____ ____

____ ____ ____ ____ ____ ____ ____ ____
____ ____ ____ ____ ____ ____ ____ ____

____ ____ ____ ____ ____ ____ ____ ____
____ ____ ____ ____ ____ ____ ____ ____

____ ____ ____ ____ ____ ____ ____ ____
____ ____ ____ ____ ____ ____ ____ ____

Baladi Solo

For each 2 line phrase, listen and repeat twice.

TKT	K	P	K	TKT	K	P	K
TKT	K	P	K	D	D	P	*

P	K	TKT	K	P	K	P	K
P	K	TKT	K	D	K	P	*

P	TKT	K	P	TKT	K	P	TKT
K	P	TKT	K	D	K	P	*

T K	T K	T K	T K	T K	T K	S	*
*	D D	D D	D D	S	*	*	*

*	KTK	T K	T K	S	KTK	T K	T K
S	KTK	T K	T K	D	K	P	*

TKT	KTK	TKT	KTK	TKT	KTK	TKT	KTK
S	D	T K	D	D	K	P	*

S	T K	T K	S	T K	T K	S	TK
T K	S	T K	T K	D	K	TKT	K

P	T K	T	P	T K	T	P	T K
T	P	T K	T	D	K	TKT	K

T ~	T K	T ~	T K	T ~	T K	T ~	T K
D	K	T K	T K	D K	D	P	K

T ~	T K	T K	T ~	T K	T K	T ~	T K
T K	T ~	T K	T K	D K	D	P	*

Make Up Your Own Baladi Solo   Track 69
Play your original phrases over the bass and riq groove!

Karsilama Solo   Track 70

For each 2 line phrase, listen and repeat twice.

T	T K	T	T K	T	T K	T K	T	T K
T	T K	T	T K	T	T K	T K	S	*

P	K	P	K	P	K	P	P	K
P	K	P	K	P	K	K	S	*

T ~	T K	T ~	T K	T ~	T K	T ~	T K	T ~
T K	T ~	T K	T ~	T K	T ~	T K	T ~	T K

P	K	K	P	K	K	P	K	K
P	K	K	P	K	K	P	K	K

TKT	K	TKT	K	TKT	K	TKT	K	TKT
K	TKT	K	TKT	K	TKT	K	TKT	K

D	P	K	P	D	T K	D	P	T K
D K	D	K	P	D	T K	D	P	T K

D ~	T K	T K	D ~	T K	T K	D ~	T K	T K
D ~	T K	T K	D ~	T K	T K	D ~	T K	T K

T K	T K	T K	T K	T K	T K	T K	T K	T K
T K	T K	T K	T K	T K	T K	S	S	*

S	T K	S	T K	S	T K	S	S	T K
S	T K	T K	S	T K	T K	S	T K	T K

TKT	KTK	S	*	TKT	KTK	S	S	*
TKT	KTK	S	*	TKT	KTK	S	S	*

74

Make Up Your Own Karsilama Solo   Track 71
Play your original phrases over the bass and riq groove!

Compositions

Here are some original dumbek compositions that I wrote for my students.

Practice Tips

Play along with the notes and the CD.

Each piece has a four beat count-off before it begins.

In the duets, the two parts are panned to right and left speakers, so you can pan to one of the speakers and play the other part – it will be like playing a duet with me!

You can see which speaker pertains to each part at the top of the page.

If you play the duets with a friend it's nice to have two differently tuned dumbeks, as demonstrated in the recording (one part is played on the six peg dumbek and the other is played on the four peg dumbek).

Naughty Nine   Part A   Track 72
Left Speaker

D   *   D   *   TK   TK   T   T   TK   X2

D   D   D   *   TK   TK   T   T   TK

D~   TK   T~   TK   D   TK   T   T~   TK   X4

D   *   D   *   TK   TK   T   T   TK   X2

D   D   D   *   TK   TK   T   T   TK

D   *   *   *   TK   TK   TK   T   TK

D   D   *   *   TK   TK   TK   T   TK

D   D   D   *   TK   TK   TK   T   TK

D   TK   TK   D   TK   TK   D   TK   TK

D   *   *   *   TK   TK   TK   T   TK

D   D   *   *   TK   TK   TK   T   TK

D   D   D   *   TK   TK   TK   T   TK

D   P   K   D   P   K   D   P   K

TKT K TKT K TKT K TKT K * X4

D * D * * * * * *
D D D * * * * * * X2

T TK T TK D TK D D TK X4
TK TK T TK D TK D D TK

D TK TK D TK TK D TK TK X4
D TK S D TK S D TK S X4
S * * * * * * * *

Naughty Nine

D   *   D   *   TK   TK   T   T   TK   X2

D   D   D   *   TK   TK   T   T   TK

D~   TK   T~   TK   D~   TK   T   T~   TK   X4

D   *   D   *   TK   TK   T   T   TK   X2

D   D   D   *   TK   TK   T   T   TK

D   *   *   *   TK   TK   TK   T   TK

D   D   *   *   TK   TK   TK   T   TK

D   D   D   *   TK   TK   TK   T   TK

D   TK   TK   D   TK   TK   D   TK   TK

D   *   *   *   TK   TK   TK   T   TK

D   D   *   *   TK   TK   TK   T   TK

D   D   D   *   TK   TK   TK   T   TK

D   P   K   D   P   K   D   P   K

D   *   D   *   *   *   *   *   *   X2
___ ___ ___ ___ ___ ___ ___ ___ ___

D   D   D   *   *   *   *   *   *
___ ___ ___ ___ ___ ___ ___ ___ ___

TKT   K   TKT   K   TKT   K   TKT   K   *   X4
____ ___ ____ ___ ____ ___ ____ ___ ___

D   TK   D   TK   TK   TK   TK   T   TK   X4
___ ___ ___ ___ ___ ___ ___ ___ ___

D   D   D   TK   TK   TK   TK   T   TK
___ ___ ___ ___ ___ ___ ___ ___ ___

D   TK   TK   D   TK   TK   D   TK   TK   X4
___ ___ ___ ___ ___ ___ ___ ___ ___

S   TK   D   S   TK   D   S   TK   D   X4
___ ___ ___ ___ ___ ___ ___ ___ ___

S   *   *   *   *   *   *   *   *
___ ___ ___ ___ ___ ___ ___ ___ ___

Shlum Birthday Piece   Part A -Track 73
Right Speaker

D	* K	* K	D	T
T	* K	* K	D	T
D	* K	* K	D	T
T K	* K	* K	D	T K
D	* K	* K	D	T
T	* K	* K	D	T
D	* K	* K	D	T
T K	* K	* K	S	*
*	*	*	*	*

X8

D	* K	* K	D	T
T	* K	* K	D	T
D	* K	* K	D	T
T K	* K	* K	D	T K
D	* K	* K	D	T
T	* K	* K	D	T
D	* K	* K	D	T
T K	* K	* K	S	*

D	D	D	D	D	X4
T K	T K	T K	S	P	

S K	S K	S K	S K	S K	X4
D	* K	* K	D	T	

~ ~	T K	~ ~	D	P	X4
~ ~	T K	~ ~	D	P	

D	* K	* K	D	T
T	* K	* K	D	T
D	* K	* K	D	T
T K	* K	* K	D	T K
D	* K	* K	D	T
T	* K	* K	D	T
D	* K	* K	D	T
T K	* K	* K	S	*

Shlum Birthday Piece   Part B   Track 73
Left speaker

*	*	*	*	*	X8

D	* K	* K	D	T
T	* K	* K	D	T
D	* K	* K	D	T
T K	* K	* K	D	T K
D	* K	* K	D	T
T	* K	* K	D	T
D	* K	* K	D	T
T K	* K	* K	S	*
T K	D	* K	T K	D
T K	D	* K	S	D
T K	D	* K	T K	D
T K	D	* K	S	D
T K	D	* K	T K	D
T K	D	* K	S	D
T K	D	* K	T K	D
T K	D	* K	S	*

T K	T K	T K	S	P	
D	D	D	D	D	X4

D	* K	* K	D	T	
S K	S K	S K	S K	S K	X4

T K	~ ~	T K	~ ~	D	
T K	~ ~	T K	~ ~	D	X4

D	* K	* K	D	T
T	* K	* K	D	T
D	* K	* K	D	T
T K	* K	* K	D	T K
D	* K	* K	D	T
T	* K	* K	D	T
D	* K	* K	D	T
T K	* K	* K	S	*

Spring Fever

D	D ~	T K	T K	D	D ~	T K	T K
D	D ~	T K	T K	D	D	P	*
D	D ~	T K	T K	D	D ~	T K	T K
D	D ~	T K	T K	D	D	P	*
D k	k S	k k	S k	D k	k S	k k	S k
D k	k S	k k	S k	D	D	P	*
D k	k S	k k	S k	D k	k S	k k	S k
D k	k S	k k	S k	D	D	P	*
P	K	P	K	P	K	P	K
P	K	P	K	D	K	P	*
TKT	K	TKT	K	TKT	K	TKT	K
TKT	K	TKT	K	D	K	P	*
S	T K	T K	T K	S	T K	T K	T K
S	T K	T K	T K	D	K	P	*

TKT	K	P	K	TKT	K	P	K
TKT	K	P	K	D	K	P	*
P	K	P	K	TKT	K	P	*
S	D	S	D	DDD	D	S	*
TKT	K	P	K	P	K	P	*
DDD	D	S	D	S	D	S	*

TKT	K	P	K
DDD	D	S	D

x 2

TKT	K	TKT	K	TKT	K	TKT	K
TKT	K	TKT	K	TK	TK	T K	TK

D	* K	D	T	D	* K	D	T
D	* K	D	T	D K	* K	D	T
D	TKTK	D	P	*	D	P	*

x 4

Ein Sh'Alla   Part A   Track 75
Left Speaker

D	K D	* K	D	T	*

*	*	*	*	*	*

D K	K D	K K	D	T	*

*	*	*	*	*	T K

D	K D	* K	D	T	T K
T	K T	* K	D	T	T K
D K	K D	K K	D	T	T K
T K	K T	K K	D	T	T K

X4

D	K D	* K	D	T	T K
T K	T K	T K	T K	T K	T K

X4

88

| D | D | D | * | T | D | X2 |
| * | T | D | * | T | * | |

| D | D | D | * | P | D | X 2 |
| * | P | D | * | P | * | |

| D | D | D | ~ ~ | T | D | X2 |
| ~ ~ | T | D | ~ ~ | T | ~~ | |

| D | D | D | T K | S | D | X2 |
| T K | S | D | T K | S | T K | |

D	D	D	*	X2
D	D	D	D	
D K	D K	D K	D K	

Crescendo!!!!!!!

| D | * K | D | D | X8 |
| T | * K | D | T | |

| D | D | D | T K | S | D | X4 |
| T K | S | D | T K | S | T K | |

| S | * | * | * | * | * |

89

Ein Sh'Alla   Part B   Track 75
Right Speaker

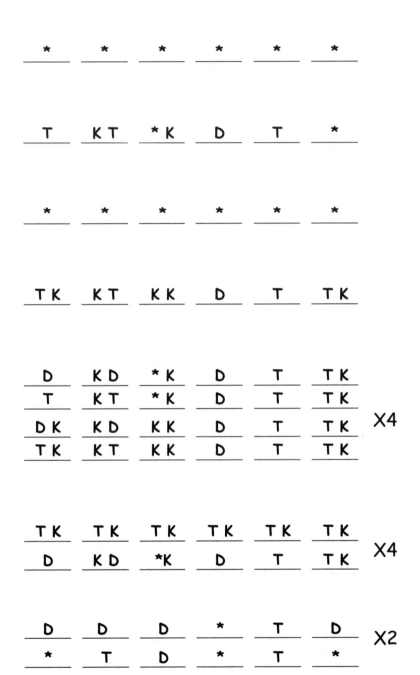

D	D	D	*	P	D	X 2
*	P	D	*	P	*	

D	D	D	~ ~	T	D	X2
~ ~	T	D	~ ~	T	~~	

D	D	D	T K	S	D	X2
T K	S	D	T K	S	T K	

D	D	D	*	X2
D	D	D	D	
D K	D K	D K	D K	

Crescendo!!!!!!!

D	* K	D	D	X8
T	* K	D	T	

D	* K	D	D	X 6
T	* K	D	T	

S	*	*	*

Track 76

Belly Dance Drum Solo Minus Lead!

This track on the CD has only the bass dumbek and riq playing this drum solo. You get to play the lead!

Malfuf - Good entrance rhythm

D k	k S	k k	S k	X 3	
D	D	S	*	X 1	X6

Masmudi -Dums give nice accents for the dancer

D	T K	D	T K	D	T K	T	T K	
D	T K	T K	T	T K	T K	T	T K	X4

Bambi - Energy drops – suspense!

| D k | k T | k k | T k | k T | k k | D | D | X 8 |

Maksum - Let the groove play four times and go off on solo phrases, repeating each variation four times. For ideas, go back to page 68 and 69. However, it's good practice to make up phrases on the spot as well.

| D | S | K | S | D | K | S | T K |

Saidi - Climax of solo – get down!

T K	D	T K	D	D	T K	S	T K	
D	S	D	D	D	T K	S	T K	X6

Zaar - Speed up into a frenzy and end with slap!

D	* K	D	T	X 3
D K	* K	D	T	X 1

Solo Ideas

Notes

If You Like Dumbek, You'll LOVE:

and their albums:

Jordan   **2005**
With Egyptian Dumbek Superstar, Osama Faruk

Dust   **2003**

Raquy and the Cavemen play progressive Middle Eastern music, HEAVY on the percussion with electrifying dumbek pieces.

These albums may be sampled and purchased through:

WWW.RAQUY.COM/CAVEMEN

The Notation Key

D = Dum (Right Hand Low Hit)

T = Tek (Right Hand Rim Hit)

K = Ka (Left Hand Rim Hit)

P = Pop

S = Slap

~ = Left Hand Finger Roll

~ ~ = Right then Left Finger Roll

* = Rest (silence)

B = Dum and Ka (Both) at same time

DD = Double Dum (When you have two consecutive Dums fast, you can play every other one with the left hand)